My Book of
THANKS

B. G. Hennessy

illustrated by
Hiroe Nakata

WALKER BOOKS
AND SUBSIDIARIES
LONDON • BOSTON • SYDNEY

Dear God...

Thank you
for me!

Help me grow strong
in body, mind and spirit.

Thank you
for loving me.

Help me remember that you are
with me wherever I go.

Thank you
for my family.

Help me to be kind
to them every day.

Thank you
for my friends.

Help me to comfort
those who are lonely.

Thank you
for time to play.

Help me remember
those who are working today.

Thank you for good things to eat.

Help me remember
those who are hungry.

Thank you for beautiful things.

Help me understand that,
in all things, beauty begins inside.

Thank you for people who teach me about your world.

Help me to listen.

Thank you
for the earth.

Help me to take care of it for you.

Thank you
for my future.

Help me remember you
in all I do.

Dear God... Thank you

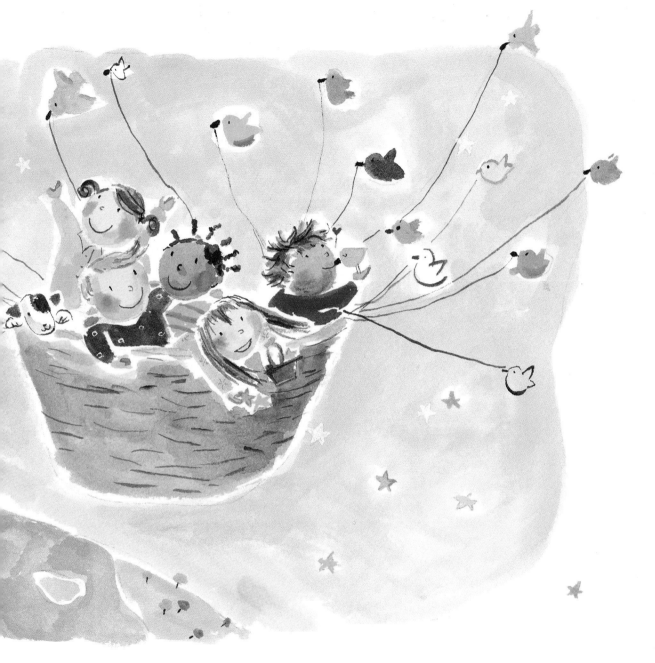

for EVERYTHING!